This book is dedic

My entire family, friends and coaches
Brenda Scorcia, Jess Scorcia, Adam Scorcia, Katie Scorcia,
Krista Scorcia, Mike Scorcia, Bobbie Scorcia, Copper Scorcia
Brady Scorcia, Irene Bloor, Fred Messacar, Mark Ellis.
The entire Etherington Family and the Motionball Team.
The Special Olympics worldwide and Chris Tampin my charity partner
and creator of this book.
Wendle Beaton for her friendship, Artistry and hard work on this book.
You did a beautiful job
Thank You I Love You All

Jason Scorcia

Chris would like to Thank The Team at Motionball, Paul Etherington and
Lynn and the gang at Special Olympics Ontario.
My entire family... my Mom Dorothy "Dolly" Tampin. My Guardian Angel
Lorraine Emma Walsh and my Love Stacey Lee Hunt.
Wendle Beaton for your undying support and hard work on this book.
Everyone around the world that believes in giving

Thank You

Christopher S Tampin

ADVOCATE KINDNESS

MEET JASON
a real life super hero

Confidence

Jason loves sports more than anything. Being shy makes it hard to join the team.

Who are the 10 most influential people in your life?

1.
2.
3.
4.
5.
6.
7.
8.
9.
10.

I am and always will be the hoper of far flung hopes and the dreamer of impossible dreams

What are 10 nice things to say to someone?

1.
2.
3.
4.
5.
6.
7.
8.
9.
10.

Being involved with Special Olympics helps Jason open up and meet new friends.

Special Olympics

Who are 10 people you would like to meet?

1.
2.
3.
4.
5.
6.
7.
8.
9.
10.

EMPOWERMENT

Jason knows he wants to give back. So with help from his friends he launches JASON'S QUEST to help kids just like him.

Even the stone you trip on is an important part of the journey

What 10 places would you like to visit?

1.
2.
3.
4.
5.
6.
7.
8.
9.
10.

Jason hears about Motionball, a charity which raises funds and awareness for the Special Olympics movement. He sees it as a dream team and joins forces.

The world is quite amazing when you're slightly strange

What are your TOP 10 favourite songs?

1.
2.
3.
4.
5.
6.
7.
8.
9.
10.

Perseverance

Jason hears about the Marathon of Sport, an epic event held by Motionball, and he wants to take part.

What are 10 things that make you HAPPY?

1.
2.
3.
4.
5.
6.
7.
8.
9.
10.

Be awesome
Be fabulous
Be remarkable
Be stellar
Be fantastic
Be you

Jason is so excited, as he is about to take part in the Marathon of Sport... He feels like a celebrity standing with the other athletes about to compete in this years event.

don't STUMBLE over something behind you

What are 10 ways to make someone feel special?

1.
2.
3.
4.
5.
6.
7.
8.
9.
10.

Jason loves to hear the cheering from the crowds. There are hundreds of smiling faces and loud applause as he enters the field.

What are 10 things you are proud of?

1.
2.
3.
4.
5.
6.
7.
8.
9.
10.

Jason loves the feeling he gets when he is competing in sporting events with his fellow athletes.

Small things done with great Love can change the world

What are 10 things you do really well?

1.
2.
3.
4.
5.
6.
7.
8.
9.
10.

Anything is Possible!

Jason embraces his courage with the power of possibility.

May you truly live all the days of your Life

~Jonathan Swift

What are 10 things you like about yourself?

1.
2.
3.
4.
5.
6.
7.
8.
9.
10.

Bravery and Courage go hand in hand. Jason thinks to himself..."I am Brave... I can do this," as he lifts his hands to greet the many high fives!

What 10 places do you love in your hometown?

1.
2.
3.
4.
5.
6.
7.
8.
9.
10.

growth

Special Olympics and Motionball have taught Jason that overcoming the challenges he has faced has made his life meaningful.

We are all pencils in the hand of GOD writing a love letter to the world

What are 10 things you love about your home?

1.
2.
3.
4.
5.
6.
7.
8.
9.
10.

Never
underestimate the
POWER OF POSSIBILITY

What are 10 things you love spending time doing?

1.
2.
3.
4.
5.
6.
7.
8.
9.
10.

Do One thing everyday that makes you Happy

What are your TOP 10 favourite TV Shows?

1.
2.
3.
4.
5.
6.
7.
8.
9.
10.

What are 10 ways to keep in shape and healthy?

1.
2.
3.
4.
5.
6.
7.
8.
9.
10.

If you had 10 wishes... what would they be?

1.
2.
3.
4.
5.
6.
7.
8.
9.
10.

the flower that blooms in adversity is the most rare and beautiful of them all

What are 10 words you would use to describe yourself?

1.
2.
3.
4.
5.
6.
7.
8.
9.
10.

What are 3 short term goals and 3 long term goals you have for yourself?

3 Short Term Goals

1.
2.
3.

3 Long Term Goals

1.
2.
3.

What are your TOP 10 favourite Movies?

1.
2.
3.
4.
5.
6.
7.
8.
9.
10.

There is Nothing More Powerful than the Human Spirit Set on Fire

Made in the USA
Charleston, SC
17 May 2016